ou ...med to any ...

Extraordinary Lives

CHARLES DICKENS

Peter Hicks

WAYLAND

First published in 2010 by Wayland

Copyright © Wayland 2010

Wayland
338 Euston Road
London NW1 3BH

Wayland Australia
Level 17/207 Kent Street
Sydney NSW 2000

Editor: Katie Powell
Designer: Phipps Design
Picture Researcher: Shelley Noronha

British Library Cataloguing in Publication Data

Hicks, Peter, 1952-
    Charles Dickens. – (Extraordinary lives)
    1. Dickens, Charles, 1812-1870–Juvenile literature.
    2. Novelists, English–19th century–Biography–Juvenile literature.
    I. Title II. Series
    823.8-dc22

ISBN: 978 0 7502 6050 3

Picture acknowledgements: Cover © Mary Evans Picture Library, p4 © Mary Evans Picture Library, p5 © Dickens Museum & Graham Salter / Lebrecht Music & Arts, p6 © Peter Hicks; p7 © Wayland Publishers, p8 © Mary Evans Picture Library, p9 © Dickens Museum & Graham Salter / Lebrecht Music & Arts, p10 © Dickens House Museum, London, UK / The Bridgeman Art Library, p11 © Wayland Publishers, p12 The Granger Collection / TopFoto, p13 © Mary Evans Picture Library, p14 © Dickens Museum & Graham Salter / Lebrecht Music & Arts, p15 © Mary Evans Picture Library, p16 © Wimbledon Society Museum of Local History, London, UK / The Bridgeman Art Library, p17 © Wayland Publishers, p18 © ITV / Rex Features Ltd, p19 © Roger Viollet /Rex Features Ltd, p20 © Peter Hicks, p21 © TopFoto, p22 © Dickens Museum & Graham Salter / Lebrecht Music & Arts, p23 © Mary Evans Picture Library, p24 © Peter Hicks, p25 © Peter Hicks, p26 © Swim Ink 2, LLC / CORBIS, p27 © Donald Cooper / Rex Features Ltd

Printed in China

Wayland is a division of Hachette Children's Books, an Hachette UK company.
www.hachette.co.uk

Contents

Words that appear in **bold** can be
found in the glossary.

Charles Dickens – an extraordinary writer

On 9 June 1865, a man and two female companions were travelling on the 14.38 train from Folkestone to London. Just after 15.00, they approached a **viaduct** over the River Beult, near Staplehurst in Kent. The line was being repaired and the removal of track had left a 40-foot gap. The train hit this gap at great speed and eight carriages plunged into the river.

By the time of the Staplehurst crash in 1865, Charles Dickens was the most famous novelist in the world.

Disaster!

Our three travellers were in a carriage perched dangerously over the river. The women cried out, but the man calmed them saying, 'We can be quiet and composed. Pray don't cry out'. He then jumped out of the carriage and found two guards running around in panic. He grabbed one and said, 'Look at me! Do you know me?' The guard replied, 'We know you very well Mr Dickens'. They had recognised Charles Dickens, the famous novelist.

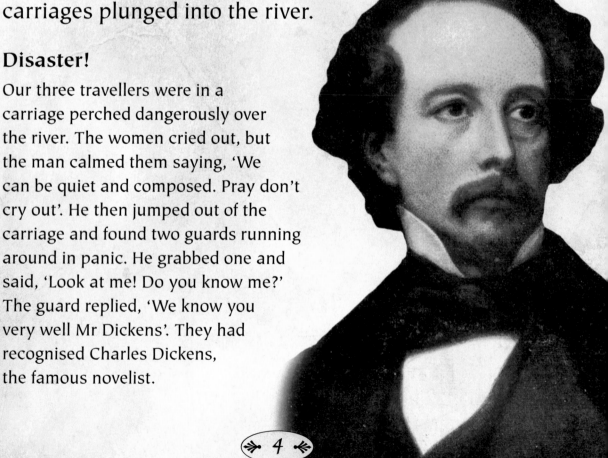

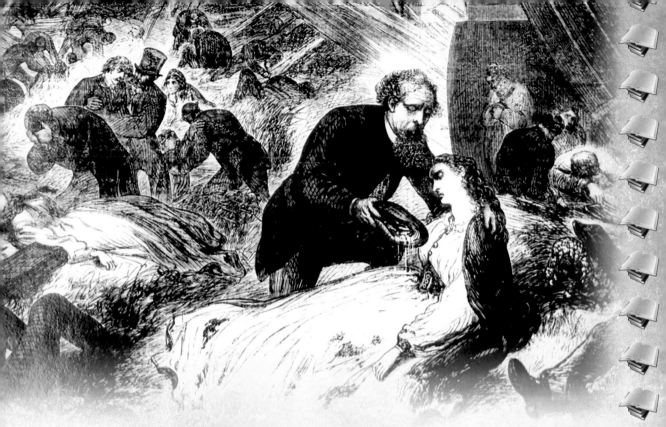

The hero

Dickens took the guard's keys and let his companions out of the carriage. He then began to help the injured and dying who were lying in, and by, the river. Dickens used his top hat to carry water for the injured to drink, and offered comfort to as many casualties as he could. Still, 10 people died and 40 more were badly injured in the crash.

Suddenly, Dickens remembered he had left the manuscript of his current novel, *Our Mutual Friend*, in his carriage. He climbed back on to the train and saved it. This disaster, and Dickens' heroic response, had a terrible effect on him. He felt sick for days afterwards, suffered from a racing pulse and panic attacks. He admitted he felt 'shattered and broken up', and his children believed he never quite recovered from the shock. Five years later, to the day, Dickens died...

This engraving is a reconstruction of Dickens helping the injured among the wreckage of the train crash.

A difficult childhood

Charles Dickens was born in Portsmouth, Hampshire, on 7 February 1812. He was the second child of John and Elizabeth Dickens. John worked for the **navy**, in the **pay office** of the large and important **dockyard** at Portsmouth. His job meant he was often moved around to the various dockyards in the south-east of England.

Here is the house that Dickens was born in at Old Commercial Road, Portsmouth.

A young boy

The young Dickens received a basic education at a day school where he developed a love for reading and the theatre. His parents took him to local theatres and to London for the Christmas pantomimes. This led to an interest in the theatre that never left him. At home, he even put on plays with his own toy theatre!

Money problems

In 1814, when Dickens was two years old, the family moved to London. Then, in 1817, John Dickens was sent to the dockyard at Chatham in Kent and returned to London in 1822.

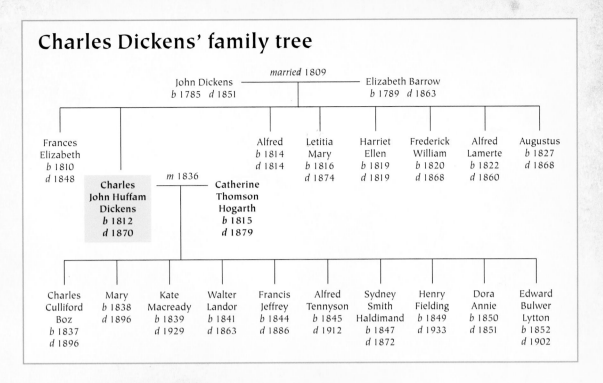

Charles Dickens' family tree

John Dickens
b 1785 d 1851

married 1809

Elizabeth Barrow
b 1789 d 1863

Frances
Elizabeth
b 1810
d 1848

Charles
John Huffam
Dickens
b 1812
d 1870

m 1836

Catherine
Thomson
Hogarth
b 1815
d 1879

Alfred
b 1814
d 1814

Letitia
Mary
b 1816
d 1874

Harriet
Ellen
b 1819
d 1819

Frederick
William
b 1820
d 1868

Alfred
Lamerte
b 1822
d 1860

Augustus
b 1827
d 1868

Charles
Culliford
Boz
b 1837
d 1896

Mary
b 1838
d 1896

Kate
Macready
b 1839
d 1929

Walter
Landor
b 1841
d 1863

Francis
Jeffrey
b 1844
d 1886

Alfred
Tennyson
b 1845
d 1912

Sydney
Smith
Haldimand
b 1847
d 1872

Henry
Fielding
b 1849
d 1933

Dora
Annie
b 1850
d 1851

Edward
Bulwer
Lytton
b 1852
d 1902

However, things began to go wrong for the Dickens family. Despite being well-paid by the navy, John Dickens was falling into debt. Between 1820 and 1824, he earned between £350 and £441 a year. In those days this was a comfortable **income**, so no one knows why he was in debt. To make matters worse, John Dickens was failing to keep up with the repayments on these **loans**. Dickens' mother tried to open a school to make some money, but it didn't attract enough pupils. Charles Dickens would have to help his family by going to work.

This family tree shows how large Dickens' family was. Dickens had seven brothers and sisters, and 10 children of his own!

CHILD WORKER

In 1824, just two days after his twelfth birthday, Dickens was sent to work because the family needed more money. His parents arranged for him to work at Warren's Blacking Factory in London. His job was to seal the lids of boot-blacking pots and stick on the labels. Dickens worked 12 hours a day for six shillings (30p) a week!

Hard times

The conditions in the blacking factory where Dickens was sent to work were grim. The floors were rotting and filthy, and rats scurried around the cellar. Dickens was given a small corner to work in, where he laboured through his long 12 hour shifts.

Factory and prison

After only a few days of working in the factory, Dickens' father was arrested for a £40 debt to the local baker. John Dickens was sent to the Marshalsea debtor's prison in Southwark, south of the River Thames. His family were eventually allowed to move in with him, but because Dickens was working, he lived in a nearby room. He had to look after himself at just 12 years of age. Lonely and miserable, he began to suffer from painful fits.

Below are the walls of Marshalsea prison. Dickens experienced two of the harshest places in 19th century Britain – factory and prison – when he was just 12 years old.

Working life

However, Dickens did make friends at the factory. Two young boys, Bob Fagin, who was an orphan, and Paul Green, helped Dickens cope with factory life. One day, when he was struck down by a fit, Bob nursed him all afternoon.

At weekends, Dickens visited his family and ran errands for his father. The Marshalsea was dirty and its walls and furniture were covered with flies.

This reconstruction portrays the difficult time Dickens experienced while working at Warren's Blacking Factory.

Freedom

The nightmare ended when John Dickens' mother died, leaving the family some much-needed money and the family were freed from the prison. At first, Dickens had to stay on at the factory as the family still needed money – there were **creditors** to pay!

One day, his father saw him working through one of the windows of the factory. John Dickens was determined that his son should return to school. Elizabeth, his mother, disagreed and wanted him to stay at Warren's Blacking Factory. Dickens never forgave what he thought was her betrayal and, from that moment, their relationship was never the same.

The world of work

Dickens spent the next two years at the Wellington House Academy in London from 1825-27. At school, he excelled at Latin and drama and amused his friends with his knowledge of 'street' language that he'd picked up while working in the factory.

Out to work

When Dickens was 15 years old, he left school and went to work for a solicitor's firm. The work was dull so he decided to become a news reporter instead. To do this, he needed to learn **shorthand**. The course normally took three years, but Dickens passed in three months!

Dickens left the solicitor's firm in 1829 and became a shorthand writer in the **Doctor's Commons** – a group of courts that dealt in church law. It was a boring job and was badly paid, but it was good experience.

Newspaper reporter

In 1831, Dickens became a reporter on the *Mirror of Parliament* – a political newspaper. He quickly developed a reputation as an able reporter.

A portrait of the confident 18-year-old Charles Dickens as he was making his way in the world of work.

CHILD LABOUR

At the time Dickens was reporting on the events of **Parliament**, many **Members of Parliament (MPs)** were worried about the huge number of children working in factories and mills across Britain. Children had to work long hours in dangerous conditions, much like Dickens had.

Small children were popular with factory owners because they were cheap to employ and could clean machinery while it was still running!

A Factory Act was made law in 1833 that stopped children under the age of nine working. It also reduced the number of hours that 9–13-year-old children could work. But with only four inspectors appointed across the country, it was hard to enforce the law.

This is a 19th century textile mill. Children were expected to work very long hours in dangerous conditions.

Becoming a writer

Dickens' journalistic career progressed during the next four years. He moved to the *True Sun* as a general reporter and, by 1833, was working for the *Morning Chronicle*. As a journalist looking for stories, Dickens gained a good knowledge of London, including where the fashionable neighbourhoods were and the slum areas, such as the 'Seven Dials', where poor people lived.

A roving reporter

His reporting took Dickens out of London, too. He travelled by coach to the industrial towns of the midlands and the north, and saw for himself how **industrialisation** was changing Britain. He saw the wealth of the factory owners, but also saw the **poverty** of many of the workers.

This engraving shows Dudley Street in the slum area of the 'Seven Dials', in London. It was famous for second-hand shoes, which you can see on display in front of the cellars.

The *Morning Chronicle's* great rival was the *Times*. Dickens loved the competition of getting his reports in before his rival journalists.

Writing to deadlines taught Dickens the need to write quickly. This was useful later in his life when he wrote his novels in instalments.

A published writer!

In 1833, Dickens got the break he needed. In December, his first story, *A Dinner in Poplar Walk*, was published in the *Monthly Magazine*. More stories quickly followed and, by August 1834, his pen name, 'Boz' was very well-known.

The stories were collected together by John Macrone in *Sketches by Boz* and were illustrated by the famous artist George Cruikshank. John Macrone, his publisher, paid Dickens £150 per volume, a lot of money in 1836. The money would come in handy, for Dickens was about to get married!

A LUCKY COLD?

While he was reporting on Parliament, Dickens had ambitions to act. In March 1832, he wrote to the *Theatre Royal* in Covent Garden to ask for an audition. A date was set, but on the morning of his appointment, Dickens had a terrible cold and could not attend. So, a common cold prevented Dickens' career on the stage and preserved him for greater things!

This is the famous title page of *Sketches by Boz*, Dickens' first book, published in 1836.

Family life

In 1830, Dickens met Maria Beadnell, the daughter of a banker. He was convinced he was in love with her and endured a difficult three-year relationship. Her parents found out Dickens' father had been in prison and thought Dickens unsuitable for their daughter. He ended the relationship in 1833.

Catherine Hogarth married Dickens in 1836. He was attracted to her dark hair and blue eyes.

Engagement

Then, in late 1834, Dickens met Catherine Hogarth, the 19-year-old daughter of another journalist at the *Morning Chronicle*. Catherine saw Dickens as an ambitious young man. Dickens thought Catherine, was beautiful and kind. In May 1835, they were engaged.

A literary career

Dickens' writing was also taking off at this time. The publishers Chapman and Hall **commissioned** him to write an amusing illustrated novel, *Pickwick Papers*, in 20 monthly instalments.

Marriage

The extra money Dickens was earning from his writing persuaded him to marry Catherine earlier than planned. He had to apply for a special license as she was under 21. The couple were married in Chelsea in April 1836. The honeymoon in Kent only lasted a week, for Dickens had to return to London for work.

On 6 January 1837, Catherine gave birth to their son, Charles. It was to be the first of 10 children! In March, the family, along with Catherine's 16-year-old sister, Mary, moved into a house in Doughty Street, London.

Number 48, Doughty Street, Holborn, London was the residence of Charles Dickens from 1837 until 1839.

A devastating blow

In May 1837, tragedy struck the Dickens family. One evening, Mary was returning from the theatre when she suffered a heart attack, dying the next day in Dickens' arms. He was devastated. The instalments for *Pickwick Papers* and the new book, *Oliver Twist*, were postponed. Dickens had inscribed on her gravestone the words, 'Young, beautiful and good'.

A social novelist

Many of Dickens' novels spoke out against issues that were affecting society, such as poverty and **sanitation**. They were also a response to the changes happening in Britain during the **Industrial Revolution**.

Workhouse and school

In *Oliver Twist* (1837), Dickens criticised the terrible conditions in many **workhouses**. People were often fed a poor diet, and some almost starved to death. In the novel, Oliver is famous for asking for 'more' food.

In *Nicholas Nickleby* (1838), Dickens wrote about the harsh treatment of pupils in Yorkshire schools. When Dickens visited the area, he found a churchyard with 34 graves of children from nearby schools. The brutality of Dotheby Hall, the school in *Nicholas Nickleby*, caused a sensation when it was published and the novel quickly sold 50,000 copies.

Charity

Dickens believed that education could help people escape poverty, so he joined the **Ragged School Movement**, a charity that set up schools for poor children.

A lady called Angela Burdett-Coutts supported and funded the Ragged School Movement.

BRITAIN'S INDUSTRIAL REVOLUTION

The Industrial Revolution was the great upheaval in Britain during the eighteenth and nineteenth centuries. Britain changed from an **agricultural** country producing food to a nation that **manufactured** goods in factories. The population grew to 20 million by 1851, and many people moved to new industrial towns and cities, leading to overcrowding.

While many people did well out of this industrialisation, such as businessmen, landowners and skilled workers, poor people suffered. The unskilled, low-paid, unemployed and old often led difficult lives in filthy slums. It was the lives of these people that interested Dickens and influenced his writing.

The Great Exhibition in Hyde Park, London, in 1851 showcased new technology in an iron and glass building, nicknamed the 'Crystal Palace', earning Britain the title 'Workshop of the World'.

A workaholic!

The 1840s were a busy time for Dickens. He wrote some of his most popular novels, such as *The Old Curiosity Shop* and *A Christmas Carol* and became a daily newspaper publisher, too.

Instalments

A big factor in Dickens' success was that his books were serialised in monthly, or weekly, instalments. This meant his readers hungered for the next twist in the plot, rather like viewers today looking forward to their favourite soap opera.
The instalments sold for a shilling (5p) a month, so people from all social classes could afford them.

Little Nell

In 1840, *The Old Curiosity Shop* was a huge success.
The story of the main character, Little Nell enthralled readers in Britain and America. Crowds gathered at New York harbour, because the last instalment hadn't reached there yet, and asked passengers from Britain, 'Is Little Nell dead?'

A still from a television adaptation of *The Old Curiosity Shop*. Many readers wept when they read of Little Nell's death, caused by the weaknesses of her gambling and debt-ridden grandfather.

America

Dickens and Catherine found time to visit America in 1842. He had an enthusiastic readership there, but wanted action on the pirating of his books (the unofficial printing of books), because America did not recognise **copyright** law. The welcome was outstanding and he and Catherine were mobbed, like celebrities, everywhere.

Further success

On his return, Dickens wrote *Martin Chuzzlewit*, *A Christmas Carol* and *The Chimes*. In these last two novels, Dickens showed his belief that Christmas could be a time for changing people for the better.

In 1846, he set up the *Daily News* newspaper, as well as published the novel *Dombey and Son*. This was followed by his masterpiece *David Copperfield* in 1849, which Dickens admitted was his favourite book.

Dickens based the character Mr Micawber (centre) in *David Copperfield* on his father. He never had enough money and was 'always waiting for something to turn up'.

Novelist and publisher

In an effort to bring his ideas about social improvement to a wider audience, Dickens published a weekly magazine called *Household Words*, in 1850. In it, he wrote about the problems of education, health and sanitation, prisons, factories and housing. He also published works by other writers, such as Elizabeth Gaskell and Wilkie Collins.

The industrial town

Dickens was interested in the factories that produced Britain's wealth, and so he visited the industrial town of Preston to get background for his next novel, *Hard Times* (1854).

This book was serialised in *Household Words*, and was so popular that it doubled the magazine's **circulation**! The book attacked the brutality of industrial Britain. It depicted factory owners caring only for money and showing little concern for their workers. It was a grim subject for a novel, and one that exhausted Dickens as he wrote it.

A photograph of Dickens with his daughters, Mary and Kate.

Prison once more

In 1855, Dickens holidayed in France and, once rested, began to write another book, *Little Dorrit*. The story re-lives the hardships of life in the Marshalsea Prison. It is a very angry book and warns against the love of money. When the Dorrit family gain riches, it does not buy them happiness, nor can they escape their past life in the Marshalsea prison.

This is the actress, Ellen Ternan. Dickens met her when they appeared together in a play called *The Frozen Deep* in Manchester in 1857.

Separation

During this time, Dickens' private life was changing, too. In 1858, he and Catherine separated. Although they had a large family, the pair had drifted apart and Dickens had secretly fallen in love with another woman, the actress Ellen Ternan. Catherine would stay in London with their eldest child, Charles, while the rest of the family would live with Dickens at Gad's Hill Place in Chatham. Catherine's sister Georgina also stayed with Dickens and became his housekeeper.

A reader and an actor

In 1853, Dickens read from his novel *A Christmas Carol* for the Birmingham Institute, a charity that provided education for working people. There was such a demand for his readings that, by 1858, Dickens was making a lot of money from reading his novels in public.

The touring author

In August 1858, Dickens began a tour of Britain. His letters to his housekeeper, Georgina and his daughters, Mary and Kate, tell of endless railway stations, hotels, halls and crowds.

His readings were well-received. Drawing on his talent as an actor, he not only read from the novels but became the characters, too. However, these readings took a heavy toll on his health.

A new magazine

Then, in 1859, Dickens closed down *Household Words* and opened *All the Year Round*. This magazine was extremely successful, possibly because of the serialisation of one of his most famous novels, *Great Expectations* in 1860-61.

Dickens somehow found the time for amateur dramatics as well as writing. Here he is with Mary Boyle in the comedy *Used Up* adapted by Charles Matthews.

RAILWAY MANIA

Dickens was able to tour England because of the massive expansion of Britain's railways in the 1840s and 1850s. More than 7,000 miles of track were laid, linking up all the major centres of population and industry.

Large areas of towns and cities were cleared to make way for train stations, while in London massive railway termini, such as King's Cross, Paddington and Euston, were additions to the capital's skyline. A vast army of labourers, called navvies (short for navigators) built a huge **infrastructure** of bridges, embankments, tunnels, **railway cuttings** and viaducts that could be seen all around the country.

This is the construction of the Brantham bridge and railway cutting on the Great Eastern Railway in Essex.

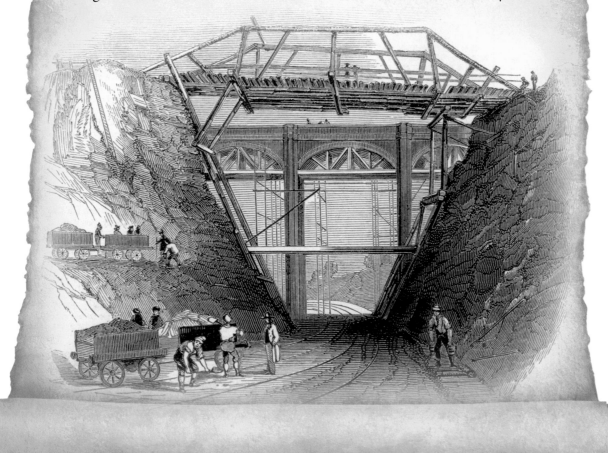

Dickens' final years

The autumn tour of 1861, which involved 50 readings around the country, was a huge success but it left Dickens exhausted. The tour finished in January 1862 and after a short break at his home Gad's Hill, Dickens returned to London for yet more readings.

This is a photograph of Dickens in his final years. Friends were worried about how tired and exhausted he looked.

Money for dirt

In November 1863, Dickens began writing *Our Mutual Friend*, a story set in the rubbish tips of London. It focused on the men who made a fortune out of the capital's rubbish. Critics pointed out that perhaps Dickens was making a comment on Britain's Industrial Revolution, which created great wealth out of dirt and grime.

More readings

Incredibly, plans were made for another tour in 1866. By this time, the strain of so many tours was taking its toll.

Dickens began to sleep badly and lose his appetite. After the Staplehurst crash in 1865 (see pages 4–5), the constant travelling by train increased his nervousness, too.

America again

Despite these health problems, and against the advice of many friends, in November 1867, Dickens set off on another reading tour of America, returning the following May. The tour was a success and Dickens made an enormous £20,000! But, it was at a huge cost to his health.

In the 1868, Dickens brought into his 'act' the murder of Nancy from *Oliver Twist*. The scene was physically demanding and left Dickens drained. He was also working on his latest novel, *The Mystery of Edwin Drood*. But, in June 1870, Dickens collapsed, losing consciousness. On 9 June, he suffered a massive stroke and died. Dickens was 58 years old. *Edwin Drood* was never completed.

WORRIES

Dickens worried about how to keep his relationship with Ellen Ternan a secret. In fact, the companions with Dickens in the Staplehurst crash, in 1865, were Ellen and her mother. It seems that Dickens never fully recovered from the shock of the disaster, suffering today from what we call **post-traumatic stress.**

Here is a copy of Dickens' death certificate. The cause of death is given as apoplexy or a stroke.

REGISTRATION DISTRICT *North Aylesford.*

DEATHS in the Sub-District of *Strood* in the County of *Kent.*

Where [died]	Name and Surname.	Sex.	Age.	Rank or Profession.	Cause of Death.	Signature, Description, and Residence of Informant.	When Registered.	Signature of Registrar.
th 870 s Hill lace gham	*Charles Dickens*	*Male*	*58 years*	*Author*	*Apoplexy Certified*	*Charles Dickens Junt Present at the death 18 Gloucester Road Regents Park London.*	*Twelfth June 1870*	*Charles Saunders Registrar*

...FIED to be a true Copy of an Entry in the Certified Copy of a Register of Deaths in the District above mentioned.

... the GENERAL REGISTER OFFICE, SOMERSET HOUSE, LONDON, under the Seal of the said Office, the 4th day of *December* 1905.

Why is Charles Dickens important today?

Dickens' death in 1870 was a shock to the world. He had requested a quiet funeral at Rochester Cathedral, but the *Times* argued that Dickens should be buried in Westminster Abbey, alongside other literary figures. So, on 14 June 1870, he was laid to rest in **Poets' Corner**. Thousands came to pay their respects to a great writer.

A global influence

Dickens' influence has spread across the world. Novelists like George Gissing and Arthur Morrison in Britain were inspired to write about social inequality and lives ruined by poverty. In France, Emile Zola's novels of working-class life owe a huge debt to Charles Dickens. The Russian novelists Dostoevsky and Tolstoy spoke of their love of his novels. Tolstoy even learned English so he could enjoy them in their original language.

This is a poster for the 1934 Hollywood production of *Great Expectations*. A Hollywood version of *David Copperfield* was also released in the same year.

Stage and screen

Before and after his death, many people saw the theatrical possibilities of Dickens' stories. *A Christmas Carol* was a very popular play even when Dickens was alive. In 1873, a stage production of *Dombey and Son* was performed in London's West End and many have since followed. Lionel Bart wrote a successful musical of *Oliver!*, which is still performed on the stage today, and *Smike* was a musical version of *Nicholas Nickleby*.

Ever since David Lean filmed *Great Expectations* in 1946 and *Oliver Twist* in 1948, the cinema has used Dickens' novels for inspiration. The director Roman Polanski produced another version of *Oliver Twist* in 2005. Television has also made many adaptations of his most popular novels, and they are shown across the world.

The ever popular musical *Oliver!* has recently been revived in the West End of London.

Dickens' stories never seem to go out of fashion. The term 'Dickensian' is used when describing poor living conditions that cause misery, distress and abuse. Dickens' characters, wit, dramatic plots and support for the helpless continue to appeal. His criticisms of greed and cruelty are as relevant in today's society as they were in **Victorian times**.

A walk through the life of Charles Dickens

Dickens leaves school and goes to work in a solicitor's office

1831

Dickens is employed as a reporter on the *Mirror of Parliament*

1827

Dickens works at Warren's Blacking Factory. John Dickens is imprisoned in the Marshalsea prison

1836

Sketches by Boz is published

Catherine has her first child. *Oliver Twist* is published

1837

Charles Dickens marries Catherine Hogarth

1824

Dickens' family move to London

1822

Dickens' family move to Chatham, Kent

Dickens is born on 7 February, in Portsmouth, Hampshire

1817

1812

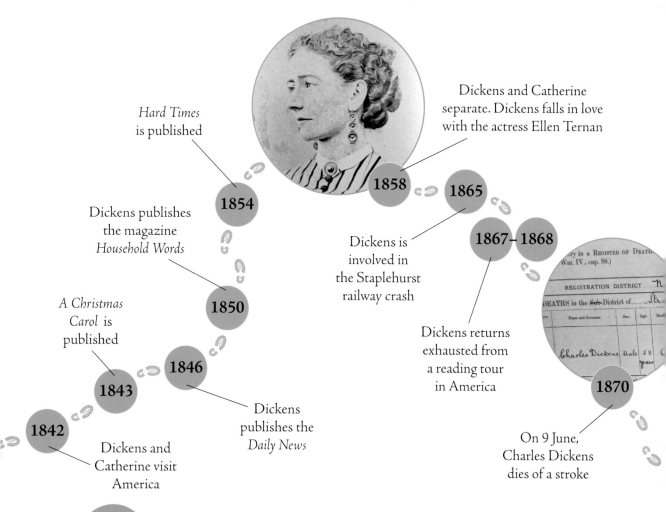

Hard Times
is published

Dickens and Catherine
separate. Dickens falls in love
with the actress Ellen Ternan

1854

1858

1865

Dickens publishes
the magazine
Household Words

Dickens is
involved in
the Staplehurst
railway crash

1867–1868

1850

REGISTRATION DISTRICT

DEATHS in the Sub-District of

*A Christmas
Carol* is
published

Dickens returns
exhausted from
a reading tour
in America

Charles Dickens Male 58 years

1843

1846

1870

1842

Dickens
publishes the
Daily News

On 9 June,
Charles Dickens
dies of a stroke

Dickens and
Catherine visit
America

QUIZ

WHAT DO YOU KNOW ABOUT DICKENS?

1. Why did Dickens' family move around so much during his childhood?

2. What factory was Dickens sent to work in at the age of 12?

3. Why was John Dickens sent to Marshalsea Prison in 1824?

4. What skill did Dickens pick up in only three months that enabled him to be a reporter?

5. Who did Dickens marry in 1836 and how many children did they have?

6. Which of Dicken' novels attacked:
   a) the misery of the workhouse
   b) poor conditions in northern boarding schools?

Answers: 1. His father worked for the navy **2.** Warren's Blacking Factory **3.** He owed a debt of £40 to the local baker **4.** Shorthand **5.** Charles married Catherine Hogarth and had 10 children **6. a)** *Oliver Twist* **b)** *Nicholas Nickelby*

Cross-curricular links

Use this topic web to explore the life of Charles Dickens in different areas of your curriculum.

HISTORY

There were some important developments in Dickens' time. Find out about:
• the Industrial Revolution
• the reform of social problems, such as poverty and poor housing.

MUSIC

Some of Dickens' novels have been turned in to musicals. Can you find out which ones?

GEOGRAPHY

• Why were Portsmouth and Chatham chosen as dockyards?
• Find out about the increases in London's transport system during Dickens' time, such as trains, bus routes, trams and underground trains.

CHARLES DICKENS

ART

Many artists have illustrated Dickens, such as George Cruikshank, Halbot Brown and Marcus Stone. Gustave Dore (who illustrated the picture on p12) is famous for his Dickensian London landscapes.

ENGLISH AND DRAMA

Have a look at some of the novels, short stories, plays and dramatic readings that Dickens wrote.

Glossary

agricultural The system of food production.

circulation The number of copies sold.

commissioned Placed an order in exchange for a fee.

copyright The legal right to control the publishing and selling of books.

creditors People or companies to whom someone owes money.

dockyard A place where ships are repaired.

Doctor's Commons A cluster of courts dealing in Church law.

income The amount of money a person earns.

Industrial Revolution The change from a society based on farming to one based on industry.

industrialisation The development of a factory system to make goods.

infrastructure The basic system of a country consisting of roads, sewers, transport networks and street lighting.

loans Sums of money borrowed from an individual, or a bank.

manufactured The making of objects by machines.

Members of Parliament (MPs) The people's representatives voted into Parliament.

navy The ships and sailors that defend a country.

Parliament An elected assembly summoned by the head of state to pass new laws.

pay office Where people's wages are calculated and distributed.

Poets' Corner Part of Westminster Abbey in London, where some of the nation's most famous writers and poets are buried.

post-traumatic stress When someone suffers anxiety and depression after a shocking or frightening experience.

poverty To live in extremely poor conditions.

Ragged School Movement A charity that provided schooling for the children of the poor.

railway cuttings When the earth is cut out of a hill so a railway line can run in a straight line.

sanitation Keeping towns and cities clean through the drainage and disposal of human waste.

shorthand A system of fast writing, using lines and symbols to represent words.

viaduct A bridge that carries a railway.

Victorian times The period in the 19th century when Queen Victoria was the monarch (1837-1901).

workhouses Places where poor people did unpaid work for food and shelter. Conditions were strict and unpleasant.

Index

Numbers in **bold** refer to photographs or illustrations.

Further Information

More books to read

A Christmas Carol (Walker Illustrated Classics) by Charles Dickens and P.J. Lynch (Walker, 2009)

Great Britons: Novelists by Simon Adams (Franklin Watts, 2007)

Victorian Life series by Liz Gogerly and Nicola Barber (Wayland, 2008)

Places to visit

- Dickens' birthplace, Portsmouth
- Dickens World, Chatham, Kent
- The Charles Dickens Museum, London

Useful websites

www.bbc.co.uk/history/historic_figures/dickens_charles.shtml
The BBC history website offers lots of information about Charles Dickens and his novels.

www.charlesdickenspage.com
This website is packed full of facts, illustrations and a timeline about Charles Dickens.

Films

- *Great Expectations* (1946 DVD)
- *David Copperfield* (BBC DVD)
- *Oliver Twist* (2005 DVD)

Extraordinary Lives

Contents of titles in the series:

WAYLAND